Fighting

Deal with it

without coming to blows

Elaine Slavens • Illustrated by Steven Murray

James Lorimer & Company Ltd., Publishers
Toronto

Do you get into

fights with people? Have you ever been so mad you felt like hitting someone? Pushing him? Punching him in the face?

All people have aggressive feelings. Have you seen a little kid hit or kick someone when they get mad? "That's mine!" they'll yell, and then *whack*! You might not see a connection between that kid and a hockey brawl or a gang fight — but It's there.

Fighting comes in many forms.

It involves a struggle of some sort and a lot of emotion. It's not just a physical act — it can be verbal, too. This book is about physical fights. Ever been in one? Chances are you haven't learned how to control your anger. Or maybe you have trouble dealing with other people's anger. Maybe you think that if you back out of a fight, you'll look like a wimp. Maybe fighting is the only way you know how to stick up for yourself.

No matter who starts it, fighting is always the wrong way out of a bad situation.

It never solves the problem and can lead to some pretty serious stuff. Truth is, uncontrolled anger can ruin friendships, make things tough at school, cause health problems, and lead to major violence. You can learn ways manage negative feelings — yours or someone else's — without fighting.

Read on to find out about what triggers anger, ways to deal with fighting, and how to be in control.

Contents

So we've all been there, right?...

Hurt or rejected

At the wrong end of a bite, hit, scratch, kick, grab, punch, or poke. Maybe you've done those things to someone else. Okay, so that's what a fight looks like once it's underway. But fights don't just come out of nowhere. The trouble begins when someone feels •••

Put down or embarrassed

Angry or annoyed

Blamed or criticized

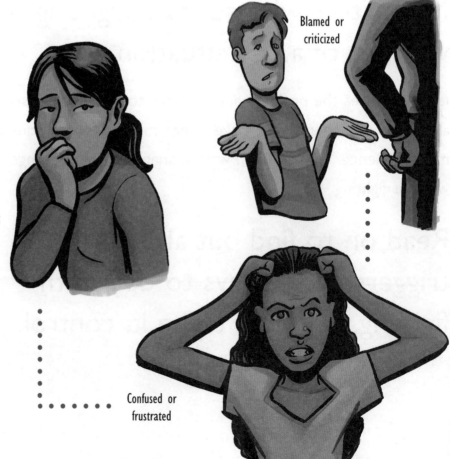

Jealous or paranoid

Scared or stressed out

Confused or frustrated

4

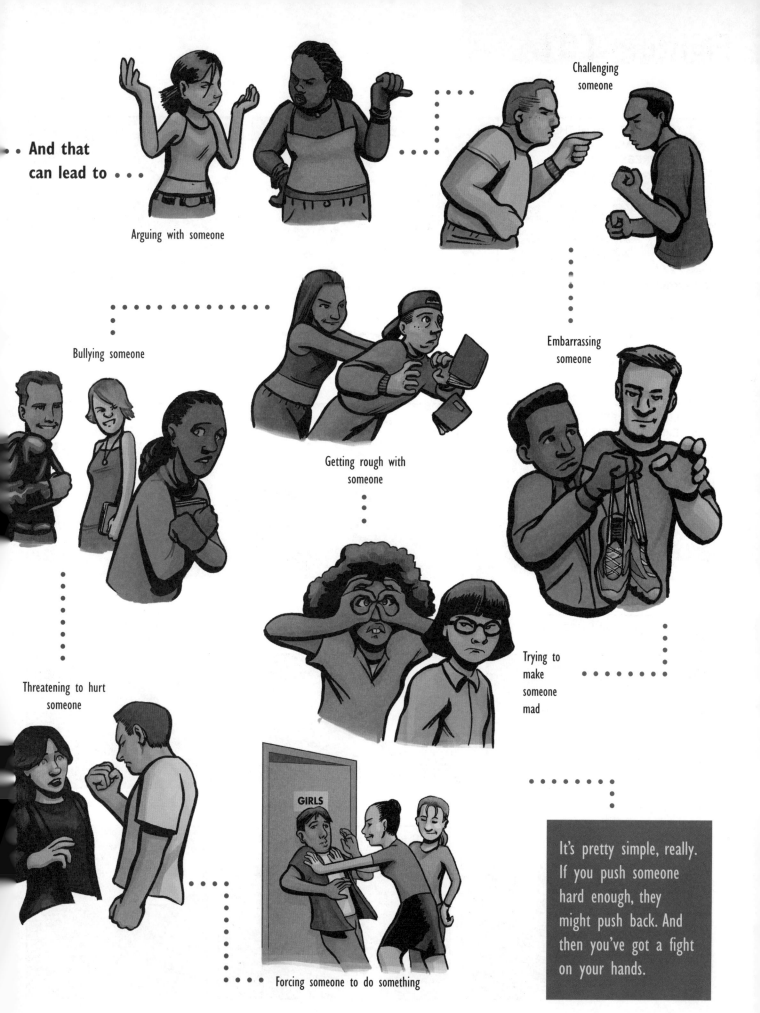

And that can lead to . . .

Arguing with someone

Challenging someone

Bullying someone

Getting rough with someone

Embarrassing someone

Threatening to hurt someone

Trying to make someone mad

Forcing someone to do something

GIRLS

It's pretty simple, really. If you push someone hard enough, they might push back. And then you've got a fight on your hands.

Fighting 101

THE TOP TEAMS IN THE LEAGUE ARE PLAYING AND THE PRESSURE'S ON...

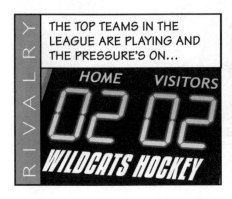

Hey!

I saw that, creep!

It always starts somewh

BULLYING

MICHAEL'S FRIENDS HARASS JAMIE EVERY DAY AFTER SCHOOL...

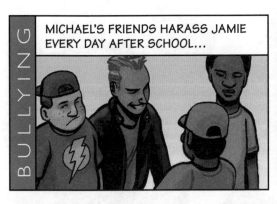

Thanks, buddy!

SOMETIMES MICHAEL WISHES THEY WOULD JUST LEAVE THE KID ALONE.

FEUDS

TARA AND MAYA USED TO BE FRIENDS...

UNTIL THEY HAD A BIG ARGUMENT LAST YEAR...

I hate you!

LATELY MAYA'S BEEN SPREADING RUMOURS ABOUT TARA...

Tara did what?

MISUNDERSTANDING

DAVE ACCIDENTALLY BUMPS INTO SETH...

THWACK!

... WHO HAS A REPUTATION FOR BEING TOUGH.

You trying to start somethin'?

No, man. It was an accident.

...

BUT THINGS ARE ABOUT TO GET WORSE FOR JAMIE...

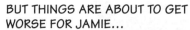

... AND TARA KNOWS IT.

NOW DAVE'S REPUTATION IS ON THE LINE...

Sure-fire ways to start a fight

BULLYING

Do you like to show people how tough you are? Back off!
Bullying makes others not want to be around you.

PLAYING dirty

Do you need to win, no matter what? Trying your best is
called being competitive. Plowing over the competition in
a game or in an argument is just plain aggressive.

TAKING revenge

It's not about winning or losing — it's about saving face. Do you get rough with people to get revenge? All you're really getting is a bad reputation.

DID YOU KNOW?

- Fighting can be an important warning sign, because teens

who are involved in physical fights often take part in other risky behaviour, such a

Carrying **WEAPONS**

When you carry weapons around, you're asking for trouble — BIG trouble. That's why schools have banned weapons and there are serious penalties for breaking the rules. Usually students are suspended and the police are called in.

Striking a **low** blow

When you diss someone, you make them angry and defensive. Throwing insults can lead to throwing punches.

BLOWING **someone off**

So a problem is beneath you? A person isn't worth your time? When you ignore someone's feelings, you can make them feel even worse, and they may decide to put you in your place.

using drugs, drinking, carrying weapons, and having unsafe sex.

- Teens who use alcohol and drugs are more likely to be involved in physical fights. Fight participants who are drunk or high are more likely to use weapons and to cause and suffer serious injuries.

QUIZ

Do you pick fights? Get dragged into fights? Totally avoid them? Take this quiz and then check out which conflict category you fall into below.

1 When you get mad at someone, do you:

A. Always say or do things you regret.
B. Try to stay cool, but sometimes lose it.
C. Calmly explain to the other person how you're feeling.

2 When you get into an argument, do you usually:

A. End up in a shouting match.
B. Get frustrated when people don't see your side of things.
C. Explain your viewpoint and listen to the other person's.

3 Does your family argue and/or fight with each other?

A. Yes, all the time.
B. We argue and sometimes my brother/sister picks a fight with me.
C. Sometimes we argue, but it never gets physical.

4 Do you ever push, hit, shove, or kick people?

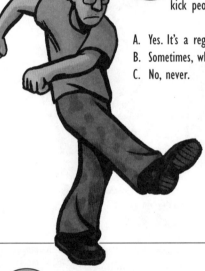

A. Yes. It's a regular thing with me.
B. Sometimes, when I have to defend myself.
C. No, never.

5 Have you ever gotten sucked into a fight or beaten someone up because your friends were doing it?

A. Yes, my group has a reputation for getting rough with people.
B. Yes, but I'm not the one who starts it.
C. No, my friends would never hurt anyone.

6 How important is it that people think you're tough?

A. Very important.
B. Sort of important.
C. Not very important.

9 Do you ever get into trouble at school?

A. Yes.
B. Nothing too serious.
C. No.

7 If you won't fight, people will:

A. Totally disrespect me.
B. Think less of me for wimping out.
C. Understand. Who wants to get hurt or into trouble?

8 When is fighting okay?

A. When you need to teach someone a lesson.
B. When you have to stand up for yourself.
C. Never.

10 Has anyone ever accused you of starting fights?

A. Yes. I have a reputation for fighting.
B. No, but I've gotten into fights.
C. No, I don't get into fights.

If you scored a lot of A's, you're an **Instigator** — the term we use in this book for someone who starts fights. It may be that you don't know another way to deal with the stuff that's bugging you.

If you scored a lot of B's, you're a **Defender** — someone who ends up in fights, but mostly to defend yourself. You may not know what to do when someone picks a fight with you.

If you scored a lot of C's, you usually manage to avoid fights, although you may have been around them. A person watching a fight is called a **Witness**.

So, who started it?

Not you, of course. It was that other person — the girl who stole your best friend. The kid who insulted you. The guy who accidentally-on-purpose bumped into you in the hall. It was that other group at school, those jerks who always act so superior and needed to be taught a lesson. People just keep getting in the way of your fists. You'd never pick a fight — would you?

DEAR DR. SHRINK-WRAPPED...

Q. I got suspended for fighting at school. My dad told the principal that I was just sticking up for myself. He said that all kids get into fights and it's no big deal. I agree!

Just Like Dad

A. Dr. Shrink-Wrapped knows that many people think of fighting as a normal part of growing up. But if you don't learn to keep your aggressive feelings in check now, what will happen later? Are you going to come to blows with your boss? Your neighbours? Your husband or wife? When a teen hits another person at school, it's called assault. Usually the student is immediately suspended and, if it happens again, may be sent to a special program for kids with behavioural problems. That may be the kind of trouble you're headed for — and it *is* a big deal. If your father doesn't see a problem with you fighting, perhaps a counsellor or a therapist can help you learn other ways to stick up for yourself.

Q. There's this girl in my neighbourhood who's like a ticking bomb — you never know when she's going to go off. She's always getting into fights and really hurts people sometimes. What's her problem?

— Ticked Off

A. Dr. Shrink-Wrapped can think of a few reasons why people may turn to fighting and violence. For instance:

- Some need to release feelings of anger or frustration. Often people who fight don't know how to express their feelings in words.
- Some need to control others or get something they want.
- Some want get back at those who have hurt them or someone they care about. They feel they have to fight to get revenge and protect themselves.
- Some feel pressure to fight from their friends, especially if they are part of a gang.
- Some are looking for attention or respect. Being aggressive makes them feel tough and important.
- Some have feelings of low self-esteem. Fighting is a way of feeling powerful.
- Some have been neglected or abused as children, or watched their parents fight. They haven't seen good examples of how to deal with conflict.
- Some have seen violence in the community. They may think it is necessary to fight to stay safe or to keep their reputations up.

Whatever the reason for this person getting into fights, what she really needs is help keeping her aggression in check.

QUIZ

Are you in control?

People who get into fights often don't know how to control their anger. Anger can be anything from feeling annoyed to full-on rage. Many people think of anger as a bad feeling. Actually, it's normal to feel angry sometimes — what's bad is what happens when anger gets out of control. You decide whether each of the following situations is an example of how anger can help you do something positive or negative. Check out the answers on the opposite page.

1 Kaleigh has worked hard on a short story assignment all week. When the story comes back from the teacher covered in corrections, Kaleigh tears it up and deletes the file from her computer. She swears never to write again.

2 Mark never says anything when he hears his friend Rick bugging someone. But he's really burned when he sees Rick push Mark's little brother into a locker and take his discman. Mark tells Rick to give his brother his discman back and to find a new friend.

3 Madeline and her sister Kat both like the same skirt at a store. They get into a loud argument about who will buy it. Madeline shoves Kat into a clothing rack. The store manager tells them both to leave and never come back.

4 Derek hates the woman his father is dating — just the sight of her makes him angry. One night he throws a rock at the woman's house and breaks a window.

5 Tara is sick of all the mean gossip at her school — often spread through anonymous e-mail addresses so people won't get caught. After her friends share a nasty message about a girl in her class, Tara tells them to cut it out or she will reveal their identities to a teacher.

6 Jason thinks the ref has made a bad call in the soccer game. The next time he passes a player from the opposing team, he sticks his foot out and trips him. They get into a fistfight, and Jason is kicked out of the game.

7 Alecia's parents won't let her go to a party because there won't be an adult there to supervise it. Alecia yells that her parents are treating her like a baby, then throws a book at the wall and breaks a vase.

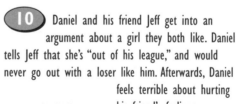

8 Tyler's teacher loves to make fun of him in class. Usually Tyler laughs it off, but he's furious when the teacher tells the whole class how badly he did on a test. After school, Tyler tells the teacher that he needs help — not jokes — to get better grades.

9 A store clerk accuses Lucy of trying to steal a sweater and checks her bag. She's livid that the clerk won't apologize for the mistake because "kids steal from us all the time." Lucy writes a letter to the store manager about the way she was treated.

10 Daniel and his friend Jeff get into an argument about a girl they both like. Daniel tells Jeff that she's "out of his league," and would never go out with a loser like him. Afterwards, Daniel feels terrible about hurting his friend's feelings.

Answers

1. Negative. If Kaleigh had cooled down and read the teacher's comments, she might have found them helpful. If she really thinks she's been treated unfairly, Kaleigh should talk to her teacher about how she could improve her mark.

2. Positive. Getting angry helped Mark to confront Rick about how he acts and defend his brother.

3. Negative. Neither Madeline nor Kat will get the skirt now, and they made a scene in a public place.

4. Negative. If Derek is upset, he should talk to his father or another trusted adult. Breaking the window didn't change anything and only leaves hard feelings for everyone.

5. Positive. Tara let her friends know how she feels about what they're doing and helped out her classmate.

6. Negative. Picking a fight with another player didn't prove anything and made things worse for Jason.

7. Negative. Throwing a tantrum won't convince Alecia's parents that she is grown up enough to attend the party, and now she may even get grounded.

8. Positive. Tyler took action when he decided the teacher had gone too far.

9. Positive. Lucy's letter may bring about a change for the better in the store's policy and she probably feels better too.

10. Negative. In the heat of the moment, Daniel said something hurtful that he regretted later. He could make them both feel better by apologizing to his friend.

How to Stop a Fight Before It Starts

There are lots of things you can do to manage your anger and put the brakes on a fight. Once you learn to recognize the warning signs, you can practice taking back control. You might try the following:

Know your body signals. Often when you start getting mad, your body gives you clues that you are about to lose control. Your heart rate increases, you get hot and flushed, and it feels like there are butterflies in your stomach. Your muscles may tense up and you might start to shake. Look down — are your arms crossed in a defensive way? Are you gritting your teeth? Having trouble thinking straight? When your body tells you you're getting "hot under the collar," find a way to cool off.

Take a few minutes to calm down. The best cure for anger, the saying goes, is time. Tell the other person that you're getting upset and need to take a break.

If you can't walk away from a difficult situation, try saying positive things to yourself — it works! When you feel yourself flaring up, tell yourself: "I can handle it."

"I can work this out."

"Things will get better soon."

"I'm not going to let this get to me."

"I can deal with it."

Get rid of all that pent-up physical aggression. Join a sport or go for a run. You could train as a boxer or take up jujitsu, a martial art that started in Japan. Not only will working out help you purge all your stress and frustration, many sports teach you to think on your feet.

To help you relax, try listening to some soothing music — or put on some hard rock, punk, or rap and tune out the rest of the world for a while. Watching movies, reading (especially something funny), or playing a computer game can help distract you from your

anger until it eases up. You should avoid TV shows, movies, and games that contain violence. Although they may not make someone fight, they do numb viewers to

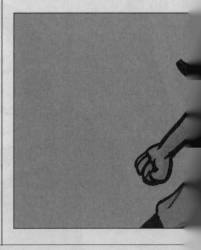

DID YOU KNOW?

- Home and school are the two most common places where kids start to become aggressive.

do's and don'ts

✓ Do count to ten and take a few deep breaths when you feel yourself getting angry.

violence and certainly won't help calm you down.

Talk to a friend, a teacher, a guidance counsellor, or someone else you trust about your problems. It can be hard to ask for help, but you may be surprised at how understanding people can be. Just remember that you're not the first person who has had to learn how to deal with fighting. You won't be the last, and you're definitely not alone.

✓ Do ask for a time-out if an argument is getting out of hand.

✓ Do say positive things to yourself.

✓ Do distract yourself by doing something else until you calm down.

✓ Do imagine yourself somewhere that makes you feel relaxed.

✓ Do think about what may happen if you fight.

✓ Do try to think clearly.

✓ Do talk to someone you trust if you're having problems.

✗ Don't try to force people to do what you want.

✗ Don't hang around with people who like to get into fights.

✗ Don't give up if you slip into old habits — keep trying.

- Aggressive children are often very popular with both friends and teachers, and have unrealistically high self-esteem.

- Aggressive children often see themselves as less aggressive, more popular, smarter, and friendlier than other people rate them.

So you're just hanging out, minding your own business.

Or you're arguing with someone and things are starting to heat up. Or you've got something that someone else wants. You didn't mean for things to come to blows, but now someone wants to fight you.

How are you going to defend yourself?

do's and don'ts

✓ Do stay away from people who get into fights.

✓ Do steer clear of bullies.

✓ Do remember that there are alternatives to fighting, like talking things out.

✓ Do try to understand the other person's viewpoint during an argument.

✓ Do state your limits. Let people know when something is bothering you and how you would like to be treated.

✓ Do avoid being alone if you know someone wants to fight you.

✓ Do ignore or walk away from a person who challenges you to a fight.

✓ Do seek help from an adult or someone else you trust, especially if you think you may be in danger.

✗ Don't provoke someone who may start a fight. If an argument is getting heated, change the subject.

✗ Don't let your friends talk you into a fight.

✗ Don't get into a fight just to preserve your reputation!

✗ Don't fight back if you can leave and/or get help.

The **Defender**

You don't have to fight just because someone wants you to.

Try these tricks the next time someone gives you a hard time.

Don't go there

Avoid getting into arguments or confrontations with people who get into fights. If you do argue with someone, stay calm, listen to their viewpoint, and look for signs that the other person is getting upset. If the argument is getting out of hand, end it. It helps to show understanding. For example: "I can understand why you're upset. I wouldn't want someone to come on to my boyfriend."

Apologize

If you've done something to make a person upset enough to pick a fight, an apology can go really far in helping hurt feelings. If there's been a misunderstanding, set the record straight: "I like your boyfriend, but I'd never take him away from you."

Offer a way out

The other person may not really want to fight you — they might just want to scare you or try to embarrass you. Don't call their bluff! Offer another solution to the problem. For example: "Why don't we just let Mike decide?" Sometimes humour can help defuse the situation. Tell them, "You're right. You could probably knock me out."

DID YOU KNOW?

- Children will have witnessed **8,000** murders and more than **100,000** other acts of violence in the media by the ti they leave elementary school.

Walk away

If someone is becoming violent, the most important thing is to stay safe. Tell the other person that you both need to take a break from the situation. You might worry that people will think you're too chicken to fight, but there's nothing cool about getting hurt.

Find strength in numbers

Try to find a teacher or another adult or join up with some friends. Avoid being alone until the person who wants to fight you has gone away or has calmed down.

- Physical fighting decreases with age. In 2001, **27%** of Grade 12 students reported being in a physical fight, compared to **40%** of Grade 9 students.

- Despite fighting, most siblings end up as good friends as adults.

Dear Conflict Counsellor

Q. My little sister fights for the computer, television, the front seat of the car, and whose turn it is to do chores around the house. Sometimes she hits, pushes, teases or threatens me to get what she wants. I don't fight back because she's smaller. How can I stop her from being so mean?
— *Big Sis*

A. Even if your sister is bigger than you, you can never solve a problem by fighting. When you're both feeling calm, tell your sister how you feel and try to work out a solution together. You might also want to talk to your parents about how your sister treats you when she fights with you and discuss ways you'd rather deal with your disagreement.

Q: Lately, I've noticed a change in my boyfriend — he argues a lot and pushes people around. I think that he is involved in a gang, and really worry that I could get hurt if I keep hanging out with him. What can I do?
— *Worried Sick*

A: You are wise to be worried about your boyfriend. Talk to him about your concerns, and if that doesn't help, suggest that he talk to a teacher or counsellor. If he refuses to go, then you need to make choices about the relationship. Your safety is the most important thing.

Q: Today at school a guy tried to pick a fight with me. The only reason I got out of it was because a teacher came by. Should I have told the teacher? What if it happens again?
— *Close Call*

A: Most schools have a behaviour code and keep a record of things like fights or threats. You should definitely report the incident to a teacher or to the principal.

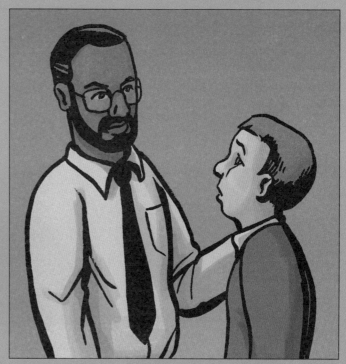

QUIZ

What would you do?

Sometimes the best way to stand up for yourself is to walk away. Other times, you might try to work things out with the other person. What you choose to do depends on the circumstances and how you feel. Think about what you would do in each of the following situations. Decide which response would best help you avoid a fight and then check your answers on page 27.

1 You want to break up with your jealous girlfriend, but when you tell her she goes ballistic and hits you. Do you:

(a) Hit her back?
(b) Tell your girlfriend that you understand that she's upset and suggest you talk about it?
(c) Yell at her that she doesn't deserve a boyfriend?

2 You miss a shot in basketball, and your team loses the game. One of your teammates pushes you around in the locker room for making the whole team lose. Do you:

(a) Kick him where it counts?
(b) Tell your teammate to shut up and get over it?
(c) Tell the coach what happened and let him deal with it?

3 Someone hears that you said something mean about her. She tells you to meet her after school for a fight. Do you:

(a) Show up for the fight?

(b) Try to talk to her about it and if she still wants to fight, tell a teacher?

(c) Tell her you didn't say those things, but whoever did was obviously right?

4 Your friends have been trading threats with a gang from another school. You hear that there's going to be a big fight between the two groups on the weekend. Do you:

(a) Tell your friends that you think the fight is a dumb idea and tell an adult if they won't listen?

(b) Decide that you will go to the fight, but will just stand by and watch?

(c) Start practicing your kicks and punches?

5 Someone demands that you give him money every week or you're going to get your face smashed in. Do you:

(a) Tell a parent, teacher or the police about the threat?

(b) Start stockpiling your allowance?

(c) Punch the guy in the face before he punches you?

Continues . . .

6 Your teammate has exchanged punches with someone from the other team. Soon, both teams are involved in a brawl. Do you:

(a) Help kick the other team's butt?

(b) Stand on the sidelines?

(c) Tell your teammates to cut it out or you'll get a coach?

8 A couple of guys get onto the bus and tell you and your friend to give them your seats — or else. Do you:

(a) Tell them you'll take "or else"?

(b) Give them your seats and get off at the next stop?

(c) Go tell the bus driver what's going on?

7 You're arguing with your sister over what program you're going to watch on TV. She tries to take the remote control from you and starts pushing and shoving. Do you:

(a) Give her the remote?

(b) Tell her she can have the remote after you decide together what you're going to watch?

(c) Tell her she'll get the remote over your dead body and give her a warning shove?

9 When you go to pick up your little brother at school, you find him fighting in the yard with some other kid. When you try to break it up, the other kid starts kicking you. Do you:
(a) Let them fight it out — kids will be kids?
(b) Give that kid the whack he deserves?
(c) Tell the kid and your brother to both stop it or you will tell their parents or a teacher?

10 Your girlfriend's ex-boyfriend has been telling people he's going to make you pay for taking her away from him. One day someone tells you that he has brought a knife to school with him. Do you:
(a) Try to talk to the guy. Maybe it's just a rumour?
(b) Tell your girlfriend and a teacher or the principal about the weapon?
(c) Start bringing a weapon to school, just in case?

Answers

1. B
2. C
3. B
4. A
5. A
6. C
7. B
8. C
9. C
10. B

You're in the kitchen,

fixing a snack. Suddenly, you hear your little brothers shouting and shoving each other around in their bedroom. Or an argument among students in your class suddenly turns violent. Not your problem, right? Better stay out of it, right? Nothing to do with you?

Well, guess again!

You can help

Of course you should avoid getting into fights, but that doesn't mean you don't have the power to stop them. Someone who watches a fight is called a witness, and witnesses have a responsibility to help ensure people don't get hurt. There are lots of things you can do to prevent or break up a violent situation without getting hurt yourself.

Peer Power

Many schools have programs in which kids act as "peer mediators" when there are disagreements among students. A "peer" is someone your own age. A "peer mediator" acts like a referee, helping people to understand each other's view of things. The point of peer mediation programs is to stop violence before it starts. The fact that so many of these programs are successful shows that witnesses can become involved in a safe, positive way. Peer mediators never get involved in physical fights, however. In that situation, their job is to get help from a teacher.

Trouble at home

Studies have shown that kids who witness family members fighting often have problems in other parts of their lives. They may:

* Feel fear, anxiety, and anger.
* Get stressed easily.
* Get sick more often.
* Get into fights.
* Have difficulties at school.

If there's fighting in your home, tell a trustworthy adult about it. This person could be a relative, guidance counsellor, teacher, school psychologist, coach, clergy member, or friend. They may help you talk to your family about their fighting or offer suggestions for things you can do to deal with it. Remember that you are your own person and do not have to make the same mistakes as your parents or siblings.

do's and don'ts

✓ Do seek help when a fight breaks out.

✓ Do tell the principal or call the police if someone is carrying a weapon.

✓ Do offer your support to someone who's been picked on.

✓ Do think about the alternatives to fighting.

✓ Do seek help if you have begun fighting yourself.

✓ Do talk to someone if a fight has upset you.

✗ Don't take part in a fight.

✗ Don't encourage people to fight.

✗ Don't hang out with someone who fights.

QUIZ

The Witness

What would you do?

No one can tell what the right thing to do is in every situation. The important thing to remember is that you almost always have choices. What would you do in the following situations? There are no wrong answers since the best solution always depends on the circumstances. Compare your answers to the suggestions given.

(1) Two girls are fighting in the school parking lot. You hear someone in the crowd watching say that it's just a "cat fight."

- Go get a teacher or the principal.
- If either of the girls is hurt, call or run for medical help.
- Tell the people watching that this is serious and the fight should be broken up.

(2) Your friend is always being called gay by a guy at school. Your friend tells you that he's sick of it and going to beat up the other guy because that will set the record straight.

- Tell your friend that people will respect him more if he doesn't let the other guy bother him.
- Explain some of the other ways to deal with problems without fighting. Remind him that he could get suspended for beating someone up.
- Tell your friend that you don't want to hang around with people who fight.
- Suggest your friend talk to someone — you, a teacher, or a parent — about how he's feeling.
- Encourage your friend to go to the principal and report the incident. Schools have human rights policies that protect students from these kinds of comments.
- Offer to stick with your friend as much as you can so he doesn't have to deal with this guy alone.

DID YOU KNOW?

A recent survey revealed that:

43% of boys and 24% of girls reported being i... a physical fight;

3 Your sister has been beaten up several times by a bully. She tells you that she's going to take martial arts so she can learn to stick up for herself.

- Talk to your sister about how it feels to be targeted by a bully. Offer your support.
- Tell your sister that it's good for women to know how to protect themselves in dangerous situations. There's a big difference, however, between using martial arts to defend against a random attack and using those skills to seek revenge.
- Give your sister suggestions on how to stay safe from a bully without fighting, such as staying near a friend or telling a teacher what's going on.
- Encourage your sister to talk to your parent. If she is reluctant, offer to go with her.

---

4 Two groups at school are always saying racist things to each other. You hear there is going to be a big fight and there may be weapons involved.

- Tell a teacher or the principal that a fight is being planned. Give as many details as you can and let them know this is a racial incident.
- If you know any of the group members, try to discourage them from fighting. Let them know that they could get hurt, suspended from school, and in trouble with the law.
- Try to understand the reasons for the rivalry between the two groups. Is there a bigger problem here that students and staff at your school need to address?
- If the two groups go ahead with the fight, call the police.

---

5 A couple of thugs tackle a guy in front of you on the street. It's not clear whether he knows them, but he is fighting back and there is a lot of shouting.

- Stay as far away from the fight as you can.
- Try to find a police officer or call 911 from the nearest phone.
- Take note of what all three men look like, in case a police officer asks you later, but keep your distance from the fight. If you know any of the men, be sure to tell the officer their names.
- If the incident has just ended, get immediate help for anyone who may be hurt. This could mean calling an ambulance or using first aid.

4% of high school students were injured seriously enough | in a fight to require medical treatment; | • fighting among youth has decreased in the last decade | from **43%** to **33%**.

More Help

It takes time and practice to learn the skills in this book. There are many ways to deal with fighting, but only <u>you</u> can know which feels right in each situation. In the end, the best response is the one that keeps you safe.

If you need more help, or someone to talk to, the following resources may be of use.

Helplines

Kids Help Phone (Canada)   1-800-668-6868
Youth Crisis Hotline (USA)   1-800-448-4663

Web sites

Bullying.org

Cyberbullying.ca

Deal.org

Health Canada – Just for You: http://www.hc-sc.gc.ca/ english/for_you/youth.html

Kids Help Phone: http://kidshelp.sympatico.ca

Media-awareness.ca

Red Cross Interactive Info for Youth: www.redcross.ca

Safeyouth.org

Stay Alert... Stay Safe: www.sass.ca

Students Against Violence Everywhere: http://www.nationalsave.org/index.php

Youthpath.ca

Youcan.ca

Books

Bullying: Deal With It before push comes to shove by Elaine Slavens. James Lorimer & Company, 2003.

Crossing the Line by A. D. Fast. Vanwell, 2003.

Danger Zone by Michele Martin Bossley. James Lorimer & Company, 2002.

Good Idea Gone Bad by Lesley Choyce. James Lorimer & Company, 1998.

Goon Squad by Michele Martin Bossley. James Lorimer & Company, 2003.

Hear My Roar: A Story of Family Violence by Ty Hochban. Annick Press, 1994.

Hit Squad by James Heneghan. Orca Book Publishers, 2003.

The Kids' Guide to Working Out Conflicts: How to Keep Cool, Stay Safe, and Get Along by Naomi Drew. Free Spirit Publishing, 2004.

The Losers' Club by John Lekich. Annick Press, 2002.

The Reunion by Jacqueline Pearce. Orca Book Publishers, 2002

Stranger at Bay by Don Aker. Stoddart Kids, 1997.

Stitches by Glen Huser. Groundwood Books, 2003.

Street Scene by Paul Kropp. Hi Interest Publishing, 2002.

Two Minutes for Roughing by Joseph Romain. James Lorimer & Company, 1994.

Text copyright © 2004 by Elaine Slavens
Illustrations copyright © 2004 by Steven Murray

All rights reserved. No part of this book may be reproduced or transmitted in any form or by any means, electronic or mechanical, including photocopying, or by any information storage or retrieval system, without permission in writing from the Publisher.

James Lorimer & Company Ltd. acknowledges the support of the Ontario Arts Council. We acknowledge the support of the Government of Canada through the Book Publishing Industry Development Program (BPIDP) for our publishing activities. We acknowledge the support of the Canada Council for the Arts for our publishing program. We acknowledge the support of the Government of Ontario through the Ontario Media Development Corporation's Ontario Book Initiative.

The Canada Council   Le Conseil des Arts
for the Arts   du Canada

ONTARIO ARTS COUNCIL
CONSEIL DES ARTS DE L'ONTARIO

Design: Blair Kerrigan/Glyphics

National Library of Canada Cataloguing in Publication Data

Slavens, Elaine

Fighting : deal with it without coming to blows / Elaine Slavens.

ISBN 1-55028-791-5

1. Fighting (Psychology)—Juvenile literature.
2. Conflict management—Juvenile literature.
I. Title.

BF723.F5S52 2004   j303.6'9   C2004-900482-4

James Lorimer & Company Ltd., Publishers
35 Britain Street
Toronto, Ontario
M5A 1R7
www. lorimer.ca

Distributed in the United States by:
Orca Book Publishers
P.O. Box 468 Custer, WA
USA 98240-0468

Printed and bound in China